Flying Lizards Big as Planes

by Ruth Owen

Consultant:
Dougal Dixon, Paleontologist
Member of the Society of Vertebrate Paleontology
United Kingdom

BEARPORT PUBLISHING

New York, New York

easy
567.91
owe

Credits
Cover, © diversepixel/Shutterstock and © Warpaint/Shutterstock; 2–3,
© Warpaint/Shutterstock; 4–5, © James Kuether; 6L, © James Kuether;
6R, © jointstar/Shutterstock; 7T, © James Kuether; 7B, © szefei/Shutterstock;
8, © public domain; 9, © James Kuether and © majeczka/Shutterstock, © Nigel
Jarvis/Shutterstock, and © B. D. S. Piotr Marcinski/Shutterstock; 10–11, © Space-
kraft/Istock Photo; 12–13, © Roger Harris/Science Photo Library/Getty Images; 14,
© Akkharat Jarusilawong/Shutterstock; 15, © Stocktrek Images/Getty Images; 16–17,
© James Kuether; 18L, © jaroslava V/Shutterstock; 18C, © design36/Shutterstock and
© michaeljung/Shutterstock; 18R, © Mark Witton/Creative Commons; 19, © Robert Clark/
Getty Images; 20–21, © diversepixel/Shutterstock and © Michael Rosskothen/Shutterstock; 21BL,
© Xinhua/Alamy; 21BR, © Chatchawal Kittirojana/Shutterstock; 22T, © Akkharat Jarusilawong/
Shutterstock; 22C, © James Kuether; 22B, © Arto Hakola/Shutterstock; 23T, © Chainarong Prasert/
Shutterstock; 23B, © Michael Rosskothen/Shutterstock.

Publisher: Kenn Goin
Senior Editor: Joyce Tavolacci
Creative Director: Spencer Brinker
Image Researcher: Ruth Owen Books

Library of Congress Cataloging-in-Publication Data

Names: Owen, Ruth, 1967– author.
Title: Flying lizards big as planes / by Ruth Owen.
Description: New York, New York : Bearport Publishing, [2019] | Series: The
   dino-sphere | Includes bibliographical references
   and index.
Identifiers: LCCN 2018049818 (print) | LCCN 2018053171 (ebook) | ISBN
   9781642802528 (Ebook) | ISBN 9781642801835 (library)
Subjects: LCSH: Dinosaurs—Flight—Juvenile literature.
Classification: LCC QE861.6.F45 (ebook) | LCC QE861.6.F45 O94 2019 (print) |
   DDC 567.918—dc23
LC record available at https://lccn.loc.gov/2018049818

For more information, write to Bearport Publishing Company, Inc., 45 West 21st Street, Suite
3B, New York, New York 10010. Printed in the United States of America.

10 9 8 7 6 5 4 3 2 1

Contents

A Flying Giant

A group of dinosaurs munches on plants.

Suddenly, they see something in the sky.

A winged creature the size of a plane swoops over them.

It's a *Hatzegopteryx* looking for a meal!

Hatzegopteryx lived about 70 million years ago.

Hatzegopteryx
(HAT-zee-gop-tur-ix)

5

Meet *Hatzegopteryx*

Hatzegopteryx was one of the biggest flying animals that ever lived.

Its **wingspan** was almost 40 feet (12 m)!

40 feet (12 m)

Hatzegopteryx

31 feet (9.5 m)

F-16 jet plane

Its head and beak were 10 feet (3 m) long.

Hatzegopteryx

Hatzegopteryx lived on Hateg Island. Today, this land is part of Romania in Europe.

A New Animal!

Scientists first discovered *Hatzegopteryx* in 1991.

They found **fossils** of the animal's skull, legs, and neck.

part of a *Hatzegopteryx* skeleton

The fossils found by the scientists are shown in red.

At first, scientists thought the creature was a dinosaur.

In fact, they had found a new giant flying animal!

Flying Reptiles

Was *Hatzegopteryx* a dinosaur—or even a bird?

In fact, it was a kind of pterosaur (TER-uh-sawr).

Pterosaurs were flying **reptiles**.

The word *pterosaur* means "winged lizard."

pterosaur

There are still reptiles today, including snakes and lizards. None of them can fly, however.

Wonderful Wings

A pterosaur had four fingers at the end of each front leg.

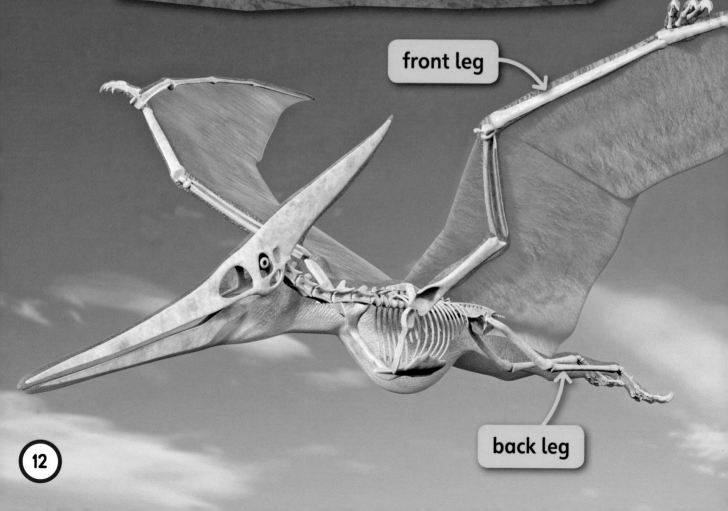

front leg

back leg

One of the fingers was extra long.

extra-long
finger

wing

A pterosaur's wings were
made of layers of skin.

Flying and Walking

A pterosaur's bones were hollow, like tubes, and lightweight.

This helped the animal fly.

The bones in a pterosaur's big skull were strong but lightweight!

pterosaur fossil

When a pterosaur landed on the ground, it stood on all fours.

It bent its wings and walked on its hands and feet.

a pterosaur called *Tupandactylus* (too-PAN-dak-ti-luhss)

Huge Hunters

What did *Hatzegopteryx* eat?

The giant pterosaur hunted dinosaurs!

It landed on the ground and crept up on its **prey**.

Scientists think it used its beak to stab its food.

Hatzegopteryx had no enemies. It was the biggest hunter on Hateg Island!

Other Giants

Hatzegopteryx wasn't the only enormous pterosaur.

A giant called *Arambourgiania* was as tall as a giraffe!

Arambourgiania
(a-RAM-bore-gee-ah-nee-ah)

Another pterosaur named *Quetzalcoatlus* lived in Texas.

It was named after a feathered **serpent** god called Quetzalcoatl.

a life-size model of *Quetzalcoatlus* (KWET-tsa-COTE-lass)

Long ago, the Aztec people of Mexico worshipped a god called Quetzalcoatl.

Taking to the Sky

Quetzalcoatlus didn't have feathers, though.

Like all pterosaurs, their bodies were covered with short hairs.

Quetzalcoatlus had a wingspan of 36 feet (11 m).

They flew through the skies at 80 miles per hour (129 kph)!

fossil eggs

Scientists have found fossils of pterosaur eggs. The eggs had soft, rubbery shells like those of alligators.

alligator eggs

Glossary

fossils (FOSS-uhlz) the rocky remains of animals and plants that lived millions of years ago

prey (PRAY) animals that are hunted and eaten by other animals

reptiles (REP-tilez) a group including dinosaurs, pterosaurs, and modern animals such as alligators

serpent (SUR-phunt)
a large, snake-like
creature from stories
that were told long ago

wingspan (WING-span)
the distance between
the tips of two wings

Index

Read More

Nunn, Daniel. *Pterodactyl (All About Dinosaurs).* North Mankato, MN: Heinemann (2015).

West, David. *Prehistoric Flying Reptiles (Prehistoric Animals).* New York: Rosen (2016).

Learn More Online

To learn more about pterosaurs, visit
www.bearportpublishing.com/dinosphere

About the Author

Ruth Owen has been developing and writing children's books for more than ten years. She first discovered dinosaurs when she was four years old—and loves them as much today as she did then!